The Household Curriculum

THE HOUSEHOLD CURRICULUM

A Workbook for Teaching Your Young Child to Think

Claudette Stock, M.A.
Judith S. McClure, Ph.D.

Photography by
W. Michel Kiteley
of
The Original Photographic Militia, Inc.

HARPER COLOPHON BOOKS
Harper & Row, Publishers
New York, Cambridge, Philadelphia, San Francisco
London, Mexico City, São Paulo, Sydney

Acknowledgments: The authors gratefully acknowledge the generous help of Gary L. LaCroix, Opal Every, Marge Morgenstern, Judy Redman, Peter Livingston, and George M. McClure.

FIRST EDITION

Designer: C. Linda Dingler

Library of Congress Cataloging in Publication Data

Stock, Claudette.
   The household curriculum.

   (Harper colophon books; CN1019)
    1. Child rearing. 2. Learning, Psychology of.
3. Domestic education. 4. Child development. I. McClure,
Judith S. II. Title
HQ769.S822   1983   649'.68   82–48805
ISBN   0–06–091019–4 (pbk.)

83 84 85 86 87 10 9 8 7 6 5 4 3 2 1

Contents

A Note to Parents

Whether your child's intelligence develops fully or not depends in large measure upon your guiding of early learning experiences before the school years. *The Household Curriculum* shows you how to take common household objects and transform them into stimulating learning tasks which develop those early intellectual building blocks so important for later, more complex, school learning.

In recent years, psychologists and educators have verified in their research what good parents have always known in their hearts—that the first, best, and most important teachers are parents themselves. Learning psychologists such as Benjamin Bloom, J. McVicker Hunt, Jerome Bruner, and Jean Piaget have conclusively established the central importance of stimulating early learning experiences in influencing children's later intellectual development. Benjamin Bloom has investigated studies of early and later learning and concludes that the growth curve for intellectual development is "negatively accelerated." By that he means the older children become, the less their intellectual development is influenced by current experience. The learning experiences children have before they enter school are of paramount importance because two-thirds of children's intellectual development has taken place by then. The more opportunities parents can arrange for their children to explore and interact with the environment, the more children touch, see, and hear, the more likely they are to develop their full intellectual capacity.

The world of young children is a qualitatively different place than the world of older children or adults. The early world of children is dominated by their senses—they know it through their hands, their eyes, their ears. They understand things with their bodies—in terms of actions—rather than more abstractly with their minds. The pieces of information gathered early about the physical world provide the building blocks for later logical understanding of the world.

A variety of sensory stimuli—sights, sounds, smells, touches—are crucial to early cognitive development. Young children who are isolated for some reason (such as those in drab, sterile orphanages) and not exposed to an adequate variety of sensory experiences are found to be retarded both physically and mentally in later life. Based on animal studies, psychologists have found that early experiences with stimulating learning tasks actually change the structure and chemistry of the brain, making it more receptive to later, more complex, learning. While studies stress the importance of adequate sensory stimulation, this does not mean that children should be bombarded with stimuli and pushed into frenzied activities. On the contrary, J. McVicker Hunt warns against overdoing stimulation when he discusses "the problem of the match." If children are given too much stimulation and pushed into too much activity, they tune out and pay no attention. On the other hand, too few stimuli and not enough activity make children apathetic and withdrawn. The ideal environment matches a child's current needs with the proper amount of stimuli and activity.

The Household Curriculum has been designed with the lessons from learning theory and research firmly in mind. Tasks are appropriately stimulating and mind-stretching but do not overstimulate or saturate. The format offers a natural yet structured approach to learning which allows parents to interact directly and positively with their children. The importance of mothers and fathers engaging in active experiences with their children cannot be overemphasized. The Swiss developmentalist, Jean Piaget, states that "intelligence is activity" and this is never truer than in early learning. At a time when the average family member spends seven hours a day watching television and just fourteen minutes a day talking to others in the household, the need for direct interaction between parent and child becomes acute. While there are excellent television programs that aid children's learning, the crucial ingredient for early learning—active participation—is missing. In an increasingly mechanical and passive world concerned parents need to plan times that will provide their young children with direct sensory stimulation and shared experiences.

Your Child's Development from Three to Five

The period from three to five years of age is a time of tremendous development for a child. He grows more skillful in managing his body, more advanced in mental abilities, and more adept at interacting with others. The typical behavioral milestones for each year are presented on the following pages. It should be noted that these milestones represent general guidelines only; each child has his own unique pattern of development. They are presented so that parents may become familiar with appropriate behaviors for each age and not ask a child to perform tasks before he is developmentally ready.

Beyond unique differences in physical and mental developmental patterns, each child demonstrates his individual temperamental style when responding to the environment. Some will eagerly plunge into activities and seek out stimulation and challenges. Others will be more cautious and require more encouragement and support. Each learning style has positive aspects and the best learning experiences are those that allow the child to use his own unique mode of interaction. Parents in their role as teachers must be sensitive to these differences so that early learning experiences remain positive and satisfying. Taking into account temperamental and developmental differences, the parents' role in guiding early learning is to provide encouragement and introduce some organizing principles to help the child define his random perceptions and add structure and meaning to his experiences.

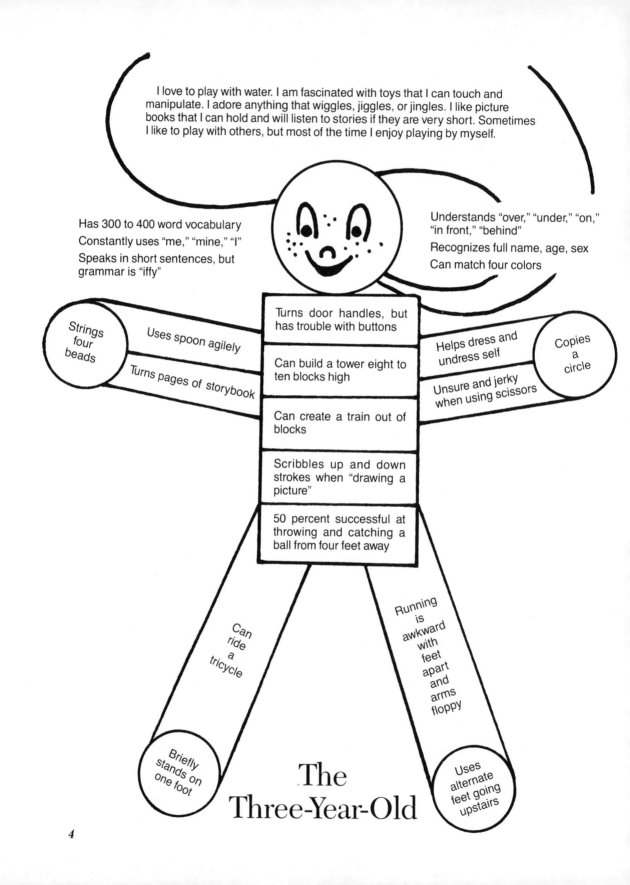

I love to play with water. I am fascinated with toys that I can touch and manipulate. I adore anything that wiggles, jiggles, or jingles. I like picture books that I can hold and will listen to stories if they are very short. Sometimes I like to play with others, but most of the time I enjoy playing by myself.

Has 300 to 400 word vocabulary

Constantly uses "me," "mine," "I"

Speaks in short sentences, but grammar is "iffy"

Understands "over," "under," "on," "in front," "behind"

Recognizes full name, age, sex

Can match four colors

Strings four beads

Uses spoon agilely

Turns pages of storybook

Turns door handles, but has trouble with buttons

Can build a tower eight to ten blocks high

Can create a train out of blocks

Scribbles up and down strokes when "drawing a picture"

50 percent successful at throwing and catching a ball from four feet away

Helps dress and undress self

Unsure and jerky when using scissors

Copies a circle

Can ride a tricycle

Running is awkward with feet apart and arms floppy

Briefly stands on one foot

Uses alternate feet going upstairs

The Three-Year-Old

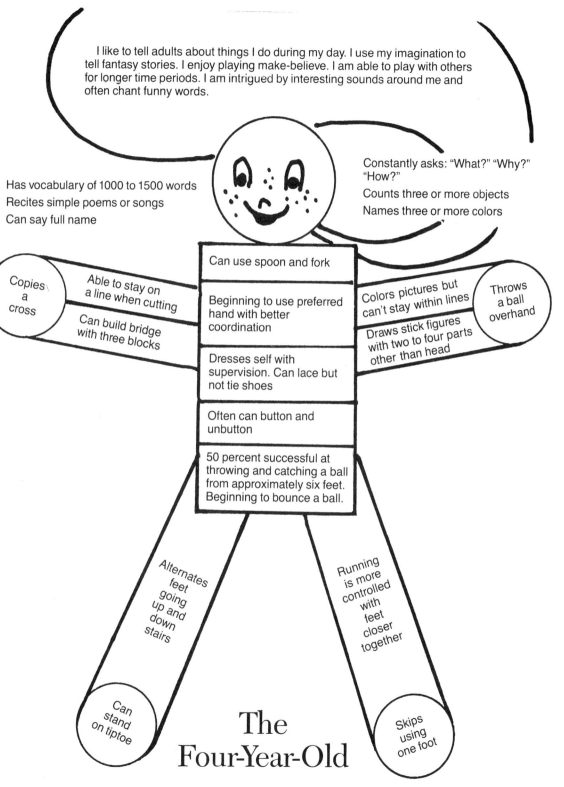

I like to tell adults about things I do during my day. I use my imagination to tell fantasy stories. I enjoy playing make-believe. I am able to play with others for longer time periods. I am intrigued by interesting sounds around me and often chant funny words.

Has vocabulary of 1000 to 1500 words
Recites simple poems or songs
Can say full name

Constantly asks: "What?" "Why?" "How?"
Counts three or more objects
Names three or more colors

Copies a cross

Able to stay on a line when cutting

Can build bridge with three blocks

Can use spoon and fork

Beginning to use preferred hand with better coordination

Dresses self with supervision. Can lace but not tie shoes

Often can button and unbutton

50 percent successful at throwing and catching a ball from approximately six feet. Beginning to bounce a ball.

Colors pictures but can't stay within lines

Draws stick figures with two to four parts other than head

Throws a ball overhand

Alternates feet going up and down stairs

Running is more controlled with feet closer together

Can stand on tiptoe

Skips using one foot

The Four-Year-Old

5

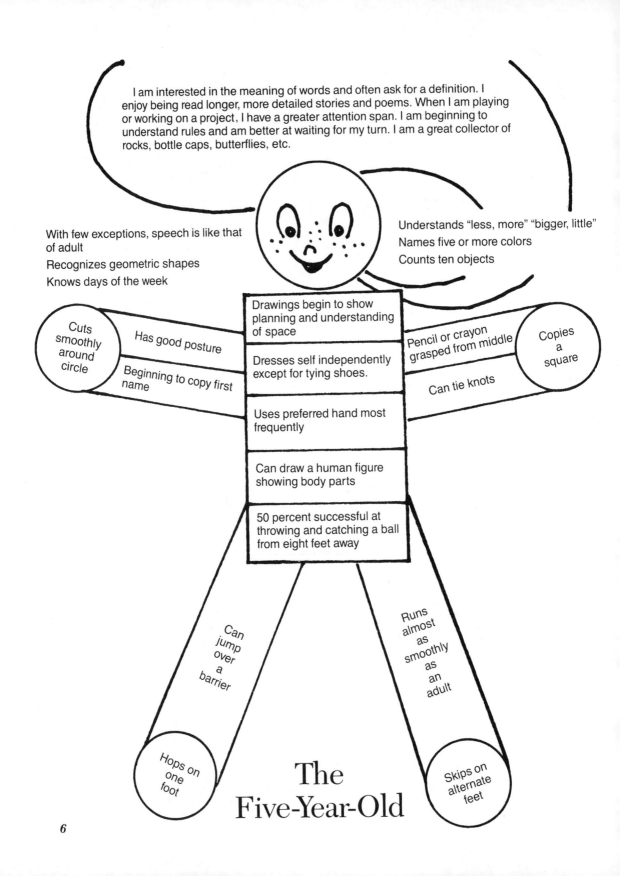

I am interested in the meaning of words and often ask for a definition. I enjoy being read longer, more detailed stories and poems. When I am playing or working on a project, I have a greater attention span. I am beginning to understand rules and am better at waiting for my turn. I am a great collector of rocks, bottle caps, butterflies, etc.

With few exceptions, speech is like that of adult

Recognizes geometric shapes

Knows days of the week

Understands "less, more" "bigger, little"

Names five or more colors

Counts ten objects

Cuts smoothly around circle

Has good posture

Beginning to copy first name

Drawings begin to show planning and understanding of space

Dresses self independently except for tying shoes.

Uses preferred hand most frequently

Can draw a human figure showing body parts

50 percent successful at throwing and catching a ball from eight feet away

Pencil or crayon grasped from middle

Can tie knots

Copies a square

Can jump over a barrier

Runs almost as smoothly as an adult

Hops on one foot

Skips on alternate feet

The Five-Year-Old

A Model for Preschool Learning

In order to use this book most effectively and confidently, it is important that you have an understanding of the different types of learning taking place.

Learning is a complex and dynamic activity of the mind that is never truly captured when reduced to formulas and models for study. However, when teaching, it is helpful and interesting to focus on the various aspects of learning involved. A useful and easily understood model for the purposes of our book is to view learning as a composite of three major processes: gathering, organizing, and using information.

```
formationinformationinformationinformationinformationinforma
tioninformationinformati                    nformationinformationi
nformationinformationinf                    ationinformationinform
ationinformationinformat                     informationinformation
informationinformationin        USING        mationinformationinfor
ninformationinformationi                     rmationinformationinfo
oninformationinformation                     informationinformation
rmationinformationinform                     oninformationinformati
oninformationinformationinformationinformationinformationinf
ormationinformationinformatio        informationinformationinfor
mationinformationinformation         ationinformationinformatio
informationinformationinfor          mationinformationinforma
mationinformationinformat            informationinformationi
oninformationinformation    ORGANIZING  mationinformationinfo
formationinformationinf              oninformationinforma
informationinformationinformationinformationinformationinfor
ninformationinformationinformationinformationinformationinfo
nformationinformationinfo            oninformationinformati
formationinformationinf              ationinformationinfor
rmationinformationinfo               ationinformationinfo
oninformationinformat                ationinformationinf
oninformationinformat'   GATHERING   informationinformat
mationinformationinfo                rmationinformationi
ninformationinformatio               informationinformati
rmationinformationinfor              oninformationinformat
informationinformationinfo           ationinformationinforma
ormationinformationinformationinformationinformationinformat
formationinformationinformationinformationinformationinforma
```

Each of the three processes involves certain skills and subskills that increase in utility and complexity as the child matures and gains experience. The processes are essentially hierarchical (see illustration, p. 7) with the use of information obviously dependent on first gathering and organizing it. Learning involves an interaction between all three processes, although different learning tasks may accentuate one or another process.

The activities in this book focus on skills in each process which are of particular importance in the preschool years.

The process of GATHERING information is the most fundamental. Here the child is physically interacting with the environment. There are three gathering skills basic to preschool learning which are emphasized in this book: attention, tactile awareness, and eye-hand coordination. Before any learning can take place the child must be able to focus *attention* on things and actions in the environment. Colorful and inviting objects used in exciting ways help to stimulate concentration and focus attention. *Tactile awareness* involves gathering information by the sense of touch. Learning to make a variety of tactile discriminations stimulates the child to make more sophisticated visual and auditory discriminations later in life. *Eye-hand coordination* is essential to manipulating objects and learning about the environment. With practice in synchronizing eye and hand movements the child becomes increasingly adept at gathering information.

ORGANIZING information requires a number of perceptual skills. This book emphasizes the most important of these skills for preschool learning: visual discrimination, auditory discrimination, spatial relationships, and directionality. As the child learns to make finer and finer visual and auditory discriminations she is learning to see and hear more subtle differences in the environment. The *visual discriminations* of particular significance for the preschool child are color, size, and shape. Important *auditory discriminations* are pitch, tone, and volume. Building up a large repertoire of discriminations in the preschool years provides a solid base for later school learning. *Spatial relationships* and *directionality* are fundamental prerequisites for reading and writing. Learning to discriminate one letter of the alphabet from another demands that the child visually discriminate shapes; learning to decode a group of letters that make up a word demands that the child see them in a specific spatial relationship. Establishing directionality is fundamental in that the child's eyes move from left to right across the page. In addition, mathematical calculations are processed up and down, as well as left and right, and right and left.

USING information is the highest-level process and requires conceptual skills. The child is involved in making higher-order associations and generalizations about the environment. Two concepts of great importance are *number* and *color*. Initially, the child can match two colors but not pick out a specific color when given the color name. Later she can pick out a color when given the name, but is not able to give the color name without a prompt. Finally, when she can accurately label an object as a specific color she is said to have developed the *concept* of color. Words which describe the environment, are themselves concepts. The importance of the preschooler developing a rich *vocabulary* cannot be overemphasized. As the child develops a variety of words to describe her experiences, she is building up categories of thought to better understand herself and the world.

An important aspect of building richer and richer concepts is the skill of *classification*. By matching, sorting, and grouping objects in her environment, the preschool child begins to develop a rudimentary system of generalization. Through better organized and structured interactions with the world the child expands and enriches her categories of experience. These are preserved in *memory* and the ability to effectively store and freely retrieve them becomes increasingly important. Not only do experiences have to be remembered, but they often need to be recalled in a particular order. Language, both spoken and written, relies on *sequential memory* to preserve the orderly relationships of sounds and symbols that produce meaning.

The skills just discussed are the skills that are systematically developed in *The Household Curriculum*. For each activity, the specific skills emphasized are listed under the heading "Focus" and are identified with the symbols illustrated below.

○ GATHERING information
    attention
    eye-hand coordination
    tactile awareness

△ ORGANIZING information
    visual discrimination
    —color
    —size
    —shape
    auditory discrimination
    spatial relationship
    directionality

□ USING information
    color concepts
    number concepts
    vocabulary

classification
memory
sequential memory

☞ The child's own hand preference should be carefully observed. Several activities have been designed with this purpose in mind, and are denoted in the "Focus" section by the hand symbol. (For further explanation of this symbol see pp.12–13.)

Guidelines for Using This Book

Each activity in *The Household Curriculum* focuses on several of the skills described in "A Model for Preschool Learning." These are listed under "Focus" at the beginning of each exercise and are coded according to the process involved. Two essentials of preschool learning are consistently practiced in each exercise: directionality and creative thinking.

However, at the same time the learning described in the model is taking place, an even more important, "invisible" learning is going on. This invisible learning is what the child is finding out about the learning process itself. If early learning experiences are enjoyable, happy times, the child will feel that learning and acquired skills are desirable and will continue to seek ways to increase his skills and find out more about his world. If, on the other hand, early learning experiences are associated with unpleasant, stressful times, the child will tend to avoid similar experiences in the future.

SIX RULES-OF-THUMB TO GUIDE YOU

1. *The first and only imperative rule for the productive use of this workbook is that both parent and child enjoy the activity and feel good about the experience and themselves.* If this is not the case, *stop immediately*, and wait for a time when the activity can be undertaken cheerfully.

2. *Advance preparation is important.* When gathering materials, think of each activity as a recipe requiring certain specific ingredients. Some must be purchased ahead of time and need preliminary preparation. Others are immediately accessible from household supplies. All the activities in the book should be scanned initially for you to become familiar with the types of items used. Materials can be gathered and organized in boxes, sacks, baskets, or other containers. The effectiveness of each activity will depend on planning ahead. Once you've decided on the activity for the day, gather the materials and select the part of the house most suitable and comfortable for enjoying it. When color, number, or size of objects used in an activity is variable, the word appears in parentheses.

3. *Do only one activity a day and keep sessions brief.* Depending on the age and attention span of the child, the session should run from five to fifteen

minutes. The cardinal rule (see #1) is to stop the session if the activity becomes a chore. *Remember the invisible learning.*

4. *Use your imagination.* The directions that accompany each activity are simply illustrative of the many variations possible. Other and perhaps more creative ideas will occur to both parent and child as they work together. Spontaneous reactions and responses to the activities should spark a natural flow of communication between parent and child. Allow this to happen and do not feel that directions must be followed explicitly.

5. *Model activities to add encouragement.* If a child is unable or reluctant to perform an activity after it has been explained slowly and carefully, the parent should model the task. Go through the activity step by step saying the directions as you do each part of the task. Often a reluctant child will join in if the adult does part of the activity and invites the child to do other parts.

6. *Let the child know that he is doing a good job.* You should constantly look for ways to comment positively during the session as well as when it is complete. Some motivating comments which encourage the child are:

"Nice work"
"You did that well"
"Good for you"
"Let's try this together"
"This time you show me"
"You really are paying attention"
"Well done"
"You're really trying"
"Here, I'll help"
"You worked hard on that"

USING OWL TO GUIDE LEARNING

Each activity has a cartoon owl next to the picture and at the end of the directions. Many children are particularly responsive to the activities if the adult gives the directions in the person of Owl. For example, Owl says, "Do you see the red bow?"; Owl says, "Put all the red bows together"; etc. While adults may initially be a bit self-conscious about using an "Owl voice," the resulting interaction is frequently magical, and not the least of the side benefits is that the adult finds she can "play" again.

Begin each activity with "Where is Owl today?" This reinforces the skill of directionality so important for later academic skills. The four concepts that you want to establish are *top, bottom, left, right.* How much the adult guides this part of the activity will depend on the child's experience. When first using the activities, the child may only point to the Owl and the adult's response would be, "Yes, Owl is at the (top) of the picture. Now *you* tell me where Owl is today." As the child learns the procedure, the adult will provide less structure for this part of the activity.

Note: The concept of left, right is a difficult one to establish and is often not well developed until later in the school years. The child's own hand preference can change several times during the early years, but by five years, a child prefers one hand or another. The adult should simply observe which hand the child seems to *prefer* using and make a mental note to try and present objects to that preferred hand. (*No attempt should be made to influence handedness.*) Simply observe and honor the child's natural preference. Several activities are particularly suitable for allowing the adult to observe which hand the child tends to use.

End each activity with "Owl asks." At the end of each activity, Owl asks the child a question to stimulate creative thinking. The adult will want to encourage as many zany, wonderful far-out thoughts as possible. Some children will plunge into this activity wholeheartedly, while others will need encouragement. The adult may want to serve as a model by brainstorming Owl's questions the first few sessions until the child gets the hang of it. Some questions will have more appeal than others, so if the child does not respond some days, don't be concerned. Another question on another day will probably tickle his fancy.

Checklist of Curriculum Materials

The materials that you will be using for activities in *The Household Curriculum* fall into two categories: common objects that are in everyday use around the house and objects which you ordinarily would discard, but will now be saving. If you don't have some of the items listed below they can be purchased inexpensively from groceries, discount stores, party shops, and secondhand stores. In some cases store samples can be obtained at no charge from local merchants.

_____ Beads, assorted sizes and colors

_____ Birthday cake decorations

_____ Bottles, plastic, assorted sizes

_____ Bows and ribbons, assorted sizes, colors, and designs

_____ Buttons, assorted sizes and colors

_____ Candies, assortment of jelly beans, gum drops, etc.

_____ Candle holders, assorted

_____ Candles and tapers, assorted sizes and colors

_____ Cardboard backings

_____ Carpet square, sample with foam rubber backing (approximately 9 in.)

_____ Chain, length approximately 1½ feet

_____ Child's clothing, outgrown

_____ Christmas decorations, nonbreakable

_____ Clothes hangers, plastic and fabric

_____ Clothesline or cord, assorted lengths

_____ Clothespins

_____ Coasters, assorted

_____ Coins

_____ Colored chalk

_____ Cookie cutters, assorted large and small

_____ Corkboard, approx. 20 in. × 12 in.

_____ Costume jewelry, assorted odds and ends

_____ Crayons

_____ Cup tree, metal or wooden

_____ Cups, plastic or paper, in varying colors

_____ Curtain rings

_____ Dice

_____ Doll clothing, odds and ends

_____ Easter eggs, plastic or styrofoam

_____ Embroidery hoops

_____ Envelopes, assorted sizes and colors

_____ Fabric, assorted scraps

_____ Feathers, assorted colors

_____ Felt marking pen, large size

_____ Film canisters

_____ Fingertip towels, matching pairs

_____ Flannel board, approx. 12 in. × 12 in.

_____ Flower arrangement holders, assorted

_____ Gift wrapping paper, scraps

_____ Glue

_____ Holiday garlands, assorted

_____ Hooks, metal or wire

_____ Houseplant

_____ Index cards

_____ Infant toys, small

_____ Key chain, bead-type

_____ Keys, assorted

_____ Kitchen utensils

_____ Knives, forks, and spoons of varying colors

_____ Lids, pet food can

_____ Macrame rings

_____ Magnets, refrigerator-type in animal, vegetable, and other shapes

_____ Margarine containers

_____ Matchboxes, empty

_____ Measuring cups and spoons, metal or plastic sets

_____ Molds, jello or salad

_____ Napkin rings

_____ Napkins, assorted distinct designs

_____ Outlet insulators

_____ Paint, small samples of

_____ Paper bags, assorted sizes and colors

_____ Paper punch, one-hole

_____ Particleboard or plywood sections, approx. 12 in. × 12 in.

_____ Pipe cleaners, large

_____ Plain white paper, 8½ in. × 11 in.

_____ Plant leaves, assorted sizes and shapes

_____ Plaques, set of 3 of varying size

_____ Playing cards, 2 decks

_____ Plastic dishes, assorted sizes and colors

_____ Pop bottle caps, plastic, in assorted colors, 2 sets

_____ Popcorn

_____ Potholders, assorted

_____ Pouch with small draw-string

_____ Powder puffs, varying in color, size, and design

_____ Rubber faucet spray

_____ Safety pins

_____ Sand

_____ Scissors, child and adult sizes

_____ Seals, assorted holiday or stationery

_____ Shoe bag, hanging plastic or cloth

_____ Shoestrings

_____ Spray can lids

_____ Spice lids, large assortment of colors and sizes

_____ Sponges, assorted shapes and colors

_____ Sponges, in form of objects

_____ Stapler; extra staples

_____ Stationery and note pads, assorted distinct designs

_____ Styrofoam or foam rubber packing material

_____ Tablecloth and napkins, paper, party-type with clear design

_____ Tape

_____ Thimbles, assorted

_____ Thumbtacks

_____ Tools, small workshop

_____ Toothpaste caps

_____ Towels, paired fingertip

_____ Tray or container approx. 18 in. × 12 in. (to hold sand)

_____ Vinyl, small samples of

_____ Wading pool or large tub

_____ Wallpaper, assorted samples

_____ Water toys, floatable

_____ Wind chimes, several, with different materials (metal, wood, etc.)

_____ Wooden spoons, varying sizes

_____ Yarn, heavy, assorted lengths

We highly recommend that you develop an easily portable box or basket that contains items used most frequently in the activities. Include:

_____ scissors, adult & child

_____ crayons

_____ marking pens

_____ cardboard pieces

_____ shoestrings

_____ yarn

_____ cord

_____ glue

_____ tape

_____ stapler; extra staples

_____ small flannel board or carpet sample

ACTIVITIES

BIRTHDAY MEMORIES

FOCUS
- ○ Practice eye-hand coordination
- △ Identify colors
- □ Count objects
- □ Develop concept of first, second, and third
- □ Label objects and shapes

MATERIALS
2 styrofoam blocks
Birthday cake decorations, assorted (farm, zoo, circus animals, clowns, etc.)
Substitute: Colored jacks or golf tees
Felt-tip marking pen

PREPARATION
Draw a straight line, a circle, a square, and a triangle on the top and bottom of two styrofoam blocks.

DIRECTIONS

Hand child several decorations.

"Where have you seen these before?" (Prompt birthday idea.)

"How old were you on your last birthday?"
"How old will you be on your next birthday?"

Place the block with the circle in front of child.

"Do you see that I have drawn a shape on this block?"
"What shape is it?"

"Yes, it is a circle, but I want you to pretend it is going to be a (farm, circus ring, etc.)."
"Let's have the (animals) parade around the circle."
"Put each (animal) right on the line."

"What is the first (animal) you choose?"
"What is the second animal?"
"Third?"

"How many (brown) (horses) are there?"

Continue as above using the different shapes.

OWL asks:
"How old are you when you are very, very old? How young are you when you are very, very young?"

HELPING HAND

FOCUS
- ○ Stimulate tactile awareness
- △ Develop spatial relationships: in front of, behind, inside of, on top of
- □ Count objects
- □ Reinforce memory skills

MATERIALS
Thimbles, assortment of at least 5
Covered container

DIRECTIONS

Place thimbles in front of child.

"Do you know why we use thimbles?" (Prompt, if necessary.)

"Put a thimble on each one of your fingers and the thumb of your hand."
"Do they feel soft or hard?"
"How many thimbles do you have? Count them as you take them off."

Place the opened container in front of child.

"Look at the thimbles carefully. Some have little pictures. Tell me what you see on each one as you put it inside this container."

"Find the one with the (bird) and put it in front of the container."

"Find the one with the (butterfly) and put it behind the container."

"Find the thimbles with the (roses) and the (hearts) and hand them to me."

"Now put the lid on and I will hand you a thimble to put on top of the container."

Empty the container and make a row of four different thimbles. (Allow child adequate time to study row.)

"Look carefully at this row. You will close your eyes and I will take one away. Look carefully."
"Close your eyes."

Remove one thimble.

Repeat as long as interest lasts.

Child may wish to reverse roles with the adult.

"Now open your eyes and tell me what thimble is missing."

OWL asks:
"What could a giant use for a thimble?"

FINGERTIP TOWELS FOR LITTLE FINGERS

FOCUS
O Develop sensory awareness
△ Discriminate patterns
☐ Count objects
☐ Establish concept of big and little
☐ Identify colors
☐ Emphasize concept of pair

MATERIALS
Assortment of paper and fabric fingertip towels that vary in color, pattern, and texture. Be sure there is at least one pair.

DIRECTIONS
Place assortment of towels in front of child.

"Look at all these little towels. How are they different from the ones you use when you take a bath?"

"What colors are the towels?"
"Pick up one of the (blue) towels."
"It's just right for your little fingers. We call it a fingertip towel."

"Do you see that some are just plain colors and some have patterns or pictures? Put all the plain colors in one pile and put all the towels with pictures in another."
"Now make new piles. Put all the towels that are the same color together."
"How many piles do we have?"

"Let's look at the pile of (orange) towels. Can you tell another way the towels are different by touching them?"

"Hand me two towels that are exactly the same in every way."
"When two things are exactly the same in every way we call them a *pair*. Please take this *pair* of towels to the bathroom and hang them up."

OWL asks:
"How do you feel when you get out of the tub and put that great big towel around you?"

UMBRELLA PLAY FOR ANY DAY

FOCUS
△ Identify pattern
△ Discriminate color
△ Match color
☐ Establish concept of same, different
☐ Develop concept of outside, inside
☐ Identify colors
☐ Count objects
☐ Match objects and number symbols
☝ Observe handedness

MATERIALS
3 umbrellas (adult and/or child), assorted
3 index cards, numbered 1,2,3
Tape
Eggs, styrofoam or plastic, in various colors
Balls, lightweight such as tennis, jack, ping-pong, indoor practice golf
Bean bag, tiny
Styrofoam base, approximately 6 in. diameter, 3 in. thick (optional)

PREPARATION
Open umbrellas and place in a cluster. One umbrella can be made to stand upright by placing tip in styrofoam base.

DIRECTIONS
(The distance the child stands from the umbrella to throw objects will vary with age and skill.)

"Where do we usually use umbrellas?"
"Why?"
"Today we're going to use them inside to play some games."

"How many umbrellas are open?"
"What colors are they?"

*Do only if using patterned umbrella.

*"Do you see one that has more than one color? What colors are in that umbrella?"

Place eggs, bean bags, and balls in front of child.

"Let's see what we have here."
"Hand me one (yellow) bean bag."
"Hand me three (blue) eggs."
"Hand me four balls."

"Look at the (yellow) umbrella."
"Find something that is the same color and toss it into that umbrella."

"Find two things that are (blue) and throw them into the umbrella of the same color."

*"Find the umbrella that is different from the others. How is it different?"

"Toss two balls and three eggs into the patterned umbrella."

"We've been thinking about the colors of the umbrellas. Now let's change the game and give the umbrellas numbers."

"Point to the numbers on the umbrellas and tell me what they are."
"Let's match each number on the umbrella with the same number of objects."
"You toss the right number of eggs into each umbrella."

°Do only if using patterned umbrella.

Remove objects from umbrellas. Tape numbered cards to handles of umbrellas.

OWL asks:
"If we only had sunny days, what would you use your umbrella for?"

27

LET'S HANG IT UP

FOCUS
○ Reinforce sensory awareness
☐ Develop vocabulary of sensory words: hard, soft
△ Emphasize color discrimination
△ Establish size discrimination
☐ Practice color concepts
☐ Count objects
☐ Develop concept of small, medium, large

MATERIALS
Clothes hangers, assorted, varying in size, color and material (Do not use wire; choose plastic and fabric hangers.)

DIRECTIONS

	"Why do we need clothes hangers?"
Hand one plastic and one fabric hanger to child.	"Feel these two hangers and tell me how they are different."
Hand child several more hangers, one at a time, to put in appropriate pile.	"Let's make two separate piles—one for hard hangers and one for soft hangers."
Continue handing child hangers, one at a time.	"Now close your eyes and I will hand you a hanger. Let's see if you can put the hard hangers in the hard pile and the soft hangers in the soft pile without looking."
Hand the child four hangers of different colors.	"Let's put these four hangers on the floor in a long line."
Point to each hanger in order.	"Tell me the color of this hanger." . . . (Prompt as necessary).
One by one, hand the child hangers that match the colors in the lines.	"Put this with the hanger that is the same color."
Repeat with appropriate color categories.	"Count how many (blue) hangers you have."

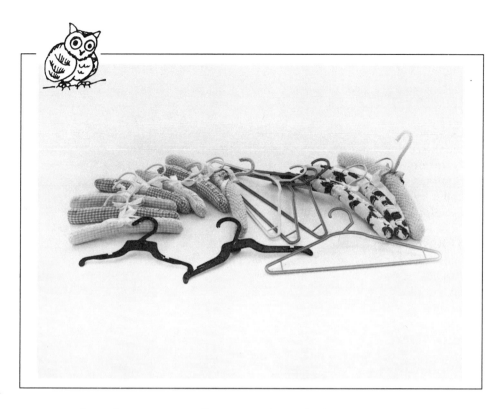

Lay out three hangers—small, medium, and large.

"Pick up the largest hanger and go hang it on the handle of the door to the (kitchen)."

"Pick up the medium-sized hanger and go hang it on the handle of the door to (your bedroom)."

"What size hanger is left?"

OWL asks:

"If we didn't have hangers, what would we do with our clothes?"

EGG PLANT

FOCUS
△ Identify color
☐ Count objects
☐ Establish concept of pair
☐ Label by color
☐ Develop concept of more and less

MATERIALS
Styrofoam Easter eggs, assorted (at least 2 of each color)
Toothpicks
Styrofoam block
Houseplant

PREPARATION
Attach a toothpick to each egg. Arrange eggs on houseplant.

DIRECTIONS

Place plant with eggs and styrofoam block in front of child.

"Colored eggs usually make us think of a special time of year—what is it?" (Prompt as necessary.)
"Today we've got a plant made of eggs and we'll play some games with them."

"Take all the (yellow) eggs off the plant and stick them on the styrofoam block."
"How many are there?"

Remove eggs.

"Put a pair of (green) eggs on the block." (Prompt if necessary.)
"How many are in a pair?"

Remove eggs.

"Put one (blue) and two (yellow) eggs on the block."
"How many are there altogether?"

Remove eggs.

"Can you find another egg the same color and put it next to mine?"

Place one egg on the block.

"What color are our eggs?"

Place all eggs in front of child.

"Are there more (less) red eggs than blue eggs?"(Prompt, by counting, if necessary.)

OWL asks:
"Where do eggs come from?"

LIVELY LIDS

FOCUS
○ Practice eye-hand coordination
△ Reinforce color discrimination
△ Develop shape discrimination
△ Establish directionality: behind, in front of, in between, on and off
□ Count objects

MATERIALS
Stuffed animal
Pet food cans, with lids
Extra lids, assorted colors. *Substitute:* Assorted potato chip, coffee, or shortening cans with plastic lids (each with a hole punched)
Heavy yarn or cord

PREPARATION
Dip one end of yarn or cord in wax to make stringing easier and knot the other end.
Put lids on cans so child may remove them.

DIRECTIONS

Place assortment of lids in front of child.	"What do we use these for?" "Pick up a (blue) lid." "Now pick up two (red) lids."
Hand yarn to child.	"You can string these lids on the yarn. Put one (red) lid on first, the (blue) one in between, and then another red one. How many lids do you have?"
Place cans in front of child.	"Take these lids off and string them with the others." "How many lids do you have altogether?"

Remove cans and place stuffed animal in front of child. Help child tie the yarn to make a necklace.

"Let's make a necklace for your (kitty)."
"You can put it around its neck."

"Now find all the (green) lids and put them behind (kitty)."

"Find all the (orange) lids and put them in front of (kitty)."

OWL asks:
"If (kitty) grew as big as this room, what could we use for a necklace?"

FRAME UP

FOCUS
○ Emphasize eye-hand coordination and tactile awareness
△ Reinforce size and shape discrimination
□ Develop vocabulary of spatial relationships: around, inside of, outside, big, little
☞ Observe handedness

MATERIALS
Small picture frames, varying in size and shape
Marking pens or crayons, assorted colors
Sheets of paper
Child's scissors

DIRECTIONS

Place frames in front of child.

"These objects are called frames. What do we put in them?"

"Where do we usually see them?"

"Do they all look the same size to you?"
"Show me the small one."
"Show me the large one."

"Let's see if they are all the same shape."
"Pick up the one shaped like a (square)."
"Pick up the (oval) shaped one."
"Pick up the (heart) shaped one."

Hand (square) shaped frame to child.

"Run your finger around the inside of the frame. Now run your finger around the outside."
"This frame is a (square)."

Put frame on a sheet of paper and give the child a marking pen or crayon.

"Take this pen and draw around the inside of the frame. Stay as close to the edge as you can."

Continue using the various frame shapes.

Select a small picture frame that will fit into one of the larger ones.

"Let's draw around the inside of this little frame, and make a picture to put inside a bigger frame."

34

Have crayons and scissors available.

"Pick your favorite color crayons and color it in."

"Now cut it out so we can put it inside the bigger frame."

OWL asks:
"If you had a magic frame, what would we see in the picture inside?"

VARIATIONS

For variation ideas the materials listed in the activity "Let's Shape Up" can be utilized nicely.

MEASURE FOR MEASURE

FOCUS
○ Practice eye-hand coordination
△ Emphasize color discrimination
△ Develop size discrimination
□ Count objects

MATERIALS
Measuring cups, plastic or metal
Measuring spoons, plastic or metal
Shoestring, knotted at one end

DIRECTIONS

Place separated cups in front of child.

"What are the names of these things we found in the kitchen?"
"What do we use them for?"

"Do they all look the same size to you?"

"Do they all look the same color?"

"Place the cups together in a nest. Start with the big one, which one comes next?"

"How many are there altogether?"

Place spoons in front of child.

"Now I want you to do something different. Start with the little spoon and put them in a row from smallest to biggest."

Hand child shoelace.

"Now let's string these together starting with the biggest. Tell me how many there are."

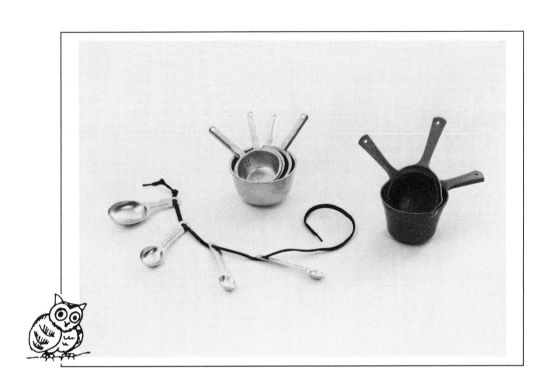

OWL asks:
"What would you do with a teaspoon of sugar?"

LILLIPUTIAN LINE

FOCUS
- ○ Practice eye-hand coordination
- △ Discriminate by color
- △ Reinforce directionality
- □ Count objects
- □ Develop concept of left and right
- □ Emphasize concepts of first, next, last
- □ Establish concept of pair

MATERIALS
Doll clothes, assorted solids and patterns, or small items of child's or infant's clothes
Child's socks and mittens
Cord or clothesline length
Clothespins, small
2 small baskets

PREPARATION
String clothesline between doorknobs, two chairs, etc., low enough to be within the child's reach.

DIRECTIONS

Lay clothing out by the clothes-line.

"Look at the clothes laid out here."
"Pick up each piece and tell me what it is."
"Tell me some other kinds of clothes that aren't here."
"Pick up what we can wear on our feet."
"How many do we need?"
"If I ask you to give me a pair of socks, how many will you give me?"
"Hand me a pair of socks."
"Hand me a pair of things that we wear on our hands."
"How many did you give me?"

Point to and describe a couple of items with patterns, stripes, etc.

"Some of the clothes have more than one color."

Place baskets near child.

"Let's use these for laundry baskets and sort the clothes. Put all the clothes with just one color in the basket on the right."
"Put all the clothes with more than one color into the basket on the left."

Remove clothes from baskets.
Point to alternate baskets.

"Find all the things we wear on our feet and put them in this basket."
"Find all the things that we pull over our legs and put them in this basket."
"Find all the things that we put our arms into and put them in this basket."

Indicate clothesline.

"Let's pretend it's a nice sunny day and we want to hang the wet clothes outside to dry in the sun. What can we hang them on?"
"First, hang up two (dresses)."
"Next, hang up one (sock)."
"Last of all, hang up two (pants)."

OWL asks:
"Go to your room and bring me your very favorite thing to wear. . . . How do you feel when you wear this?"

WATERFALL FUN

FOCUS
O Sensory awareness
□ Develop vocabulary of sensory words: soft, prickly, hard, warm, cold

MATERIALS
Rubber faucet sprayer or garden hose with spray

PREPARATION
This activity is done at a sink or outside with hose.

DIRECTIONS

Attach sprayer to sink faucet or hose. (Have child stand on stool if using the sink.)

"Do you know what this thing I've put on the (faucet/hose) is called?"

"Can you tell me how this water feels when it comes through the sprayer?" (Prompt if necessary.)

"Does it feel soft?"
"Does it feel hard?"
"Does it feel prickly?"

Change temperature of water.

"Does it feel cold?"
"Does it feel warm?"

Change intensity of water by manipulating sprayer.

"What made the water change?"
"You may move it and see it change." (Help child with sprayer, if necessary.)
"Make the water come out fast."
"Make the water come out slow."
"Does the water splash?"
"What makes the water come out the way you like it best?"

OWL asks:
"Do you think it feels like rain or snow when you put your hands under the sprayer?"

VARIATIONS
The child may enjoy manipulating the objects used in the activity "Winds, Waves, and Water" since he is already familiar with them. The child can also be encouraged to choose favorite objects that he plays with in the bathtub or wading pool.

CREATURES GREAT AND SMALL

FOCUS
○ Encourage sensory awareness
△ Emphasize size discrimination
△ Establish directionality
△ Reinforce size and color discrimination
□ Count three objects

MATERIALS
Corkboard or pegboard, approximately 20 in.x12 in.
3 objects—small, medium, and large—such as the ceramic fish pictured or plastic ornaments, fabric flowers, stuffed animals, or whatever objects are particularly appealing to the child
3 metal hooks or wire (to attach objects to board)

PREPARATION
Use the hooks or wire to attach the three objects firmly enough to the corkboard so that they don't fall off when the child touches them.

DIRECTIONS

Place corkboard picture in front of child.

"Look at the picture I've made for you. I want you to tell me some things about it. What do you see?"

"How do the (fish) feel?"

"Put your hand on the small (fish)."
"Put your hand on the large (fish)."
"Now put your hand on the medium-size (fish)."

"Are all the (fish) facing the same way?"
"Which way is the little fish facing?" (If child points adult should reinforce by saying, "Yes, the little fish is facing left.")
"Which way is the big (fish) facing?"

"How are the three (fish) different?"

"How many (fish) are there?"

OWL asks:
"If you only had two friends what great
big creature and what little bitty creature would you pick?"

LET'S SHAPE UP

FOCUS
- ○ Practice eye-hand coordination
- ○ Emphasize sensory awareness
- △ Reinforce shape discrimination
- □ Label various shapes
- □ Establish spatial concepts
- □ Label colors
- □ Count objects

MATERIALS
Styrofoam and foam pieces saved from packing boxes, different sizes and shapes
Embroidery hoops
Sheets of paper
Child's scissors
Crayons or marking pens

DIRECTIONS

Place styrofoam materials in front of child.	"I've put out some materials that are different shapes. Let's look around the room and see how many shapes we can discover." "What shape is the window?" "What shape is the table?" "What shape is the planter?"
Hand child one of the shapes.	"Trace around the inside of this (rectangle) with your finger."
Put the shape on the paper and hand child a crayon. (Adult may need to hold the object steady as the child traces.)	"Now let's draw around the inside of the (rectangle) using this as a pattern."
Repeat the two tracing directions above with other styrofoam shapes.	"Let's see if you can find an oval shape that's like an egg." "It's called an embroidery hoop." "First trace around the inside with your finger and then trace around the outside."
Put hoop on the paper and hand child a crayon. (Steady object as necessary.)	"Now let's draw around the inside and the outside of the oval." "Now that you have made an egg, let's pretend it's an Easter egg."

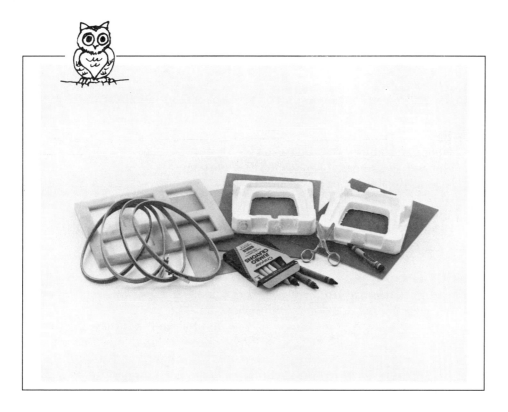

Hand child crayons.

The inside and and outside tracing of the hoop provides a large border for the child to cut on.

"Tell me what your favorite color crayons are. Pick three to color your egg."

"Now you may cut out your Easter egg with your scissors."

OWL asks:
"If our house could be any shape—what shape would you like it to be?"

RING MY CHIMES

FOCUS
△ Emphasize auditory discrimination
△ Stimulate awareness of sounds in the environment
☐ Develop vocabulary of sound words

MATERIALS
Wind chimes—at least 2—of different materials: wood, metal, plastic, glass, shells, ceramic

DIRECTIONS

Hang chimes up in front of child—over chair, doorknob, etc.	"Let's look at these pretty things that belong outside." "Can you tell me what they are?" "Why do you think they are called wind chimes?" (Prompt if necessary)
Ring the different chimes.	"Do the different chimes sound the same?" "Why?" "I was moving the chimes just then, but what makes them move when they are outside?" (Prompt if necessary.)
Ring each set of chimes, one at a time, and repeat question.	"What are these chimes made of?"

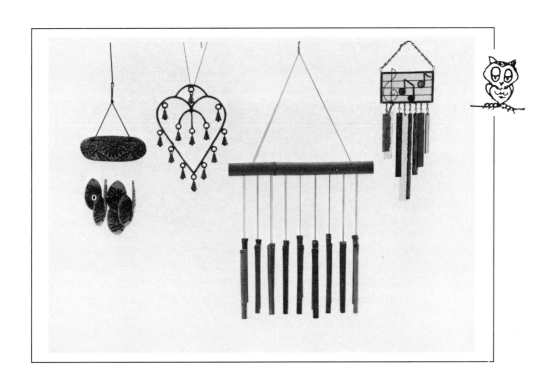

OWL asks:
"What do you think of when you hear the sound of this chime?"

PICK A POCKET

FOCUS
○ Develop eye-hand coordination
△ Reinforce directionality
□ Count objects
□ Reinforce spatial concepts: top, bottom, in, next
□ Identify number symbols
□ Develop memory skills

MATERIALS
Hanging shoebag, cloth or plastic. *Substitute:* Cloth or plastic hosiery container.
Kitchen and cleaning utensils that will fit into pockets of shoebag, or smaller items such as plastic knives, spoons, and forks if using a hosiery container (12-18 items)
Index cards
Marking pen
Paper clips

PREPARATION
Hang shoebag low enough for the child to reach.
Write large numbers 1, 2, 3, 4 on index cards.

DIRECTIONS

Hand utensils one at a time to child.

"What is this called?"
"What does it do?"

Encourage child to work from left to right. (Continue activity to more complex level depending upon skill level of child.)

"I want you to put one utensil in each pocket in the top row."

"Count how many objects there are."

"Now, put two utensils in each pocket of the next row."

"Count how many objects there are."
"Now put three utensils in each pocket of the bottom row."

Attach numbered index cards to pockets in the top row. Remove utensil after each direction. Increase number of objects depending on child's ability to remember.

"Put the (spatula) in pocket #1."
"Put the (spoon) in pocket #2 and the (egg beater) in pocket #4."
"Put the (spatula) in pocket #2, the (pancake turner) in #1, and the (fork) in pocket #4."

Randomly select pockets. If the child can't remember, limit the game to one row.

"I am going to put this (spoon) in one of the pockets."
"You look closely and remember which pocket it's in."
"Now close your eyes and I will hand it to you."
"You put it back where it was."

OWL asks:
"What would be your favorite things to hide in these pockets?"

TREE RINGS

FOCUS

○ Develop eye-hand coordination
△ Stimulate size discrimination and spatial awareness
△ Reinforce shape discrimination
□ Identify colors
□ Count objects
□ Establish concepts of size and directionality
☞ Observe handedness

MATERIALS

Metal or wooden cup tree
Rings to hang on tree, assortment of sizes and colors such as curtain, napkin, macrame, sewing, costume jewelry

DIRECTIONS

Place cup tree in front of child.	"What do we usually have hanging on this?" "Today we're going to hang other things on the tree to decorate it."
Place rings in front of child.	"Put a ring on a branch of the tree." "How many branches does the tree have?" "How many rings did you place on the tree?"
Remove rings	"Put a large ring on a bottom branch and a small ring on a top branch." "Hand me the large ring." "Hand me the small ring." "How many rings did you give me altogether?" "Are these rings square?" "What shape are they?" "Put as many (blue) rings as you can on the tree." "How many (blue) rings are there?"

OWL asks:
"Let's pretend that we are decorating the trees outside. What could you take from the sky to put on their branches?"

MAGNET MAGIC

FOCUS
- △ Reinforce directionality
- ☐ Classify by category
- ☐ Classify by color
- ☐ Experiment with the principle of a magnetic field
- ☐ Count objects
- ☐ Label objects
- ☐ Count by color and category

MATERIALS
Assorted magnets commonly used to attach papers to the refrigerator
Paper clips

DIRECTIONS

Remove magnets from the refrigerator and place in front of child.	"Today we'll do our activity next to the refrigerator." "Let's turn these over and see what it is that makes them stick to the refrigerator." "That piece of metal is called a magnet and it always sticks to iron."
Put paper clip in front of child.	"What happens when you put the magnet down on this pile of paper clips?" "How many paper clips did the magnet pick up?" "As I point to each item, let's say its name together." "Put the (tomato) on the refrigerator door. Why does it stick?" "What color is the (tomato)?" "Now put all the other (red) things next to the (tomato)."
Repeat with other items in same color categories.	
Remove all items from refrigerator and place on floor.	"Some of these things are (fruits) and some are (vegetables)."
Indicate left side of refrigerator.	"Put all the (vegetables) here on the left side of the refrigerator. As you put each one up, say its name."

52

Indicate right side of refrigerator.

"Now put all the (fruits) on the right side of the refrigerator. As you put each one up, say its name."

"Let's count how many (vegetables) we have."

"Let's count how many (fruits) we have."

"Now count all of the (red) items we have."

Repeat with appropriate color categories.

OWL asks:
"If you had a magnet as big as this room, what would you pick up?"

SANDSATIONS

FOCUS
- ○ Develop eye-hand coordination and sensory awareness
- △ Stimulate size discrimination
- △ Reinforce spatial awareness
- △ Discriminate shapes: line, circle
- □ Count objects
- □ Emphasize concept of first and last
- □ Establish concept of small, medium, large

MATERIALS
Cookie cutters, small, medium, and large of the same designs
Wooden spoons, a set of varying sizes
Jello or salad molds, at least one
Strainer
Plastic spatula

PREPARATION
Do activity in sandbox or fill a large sturdy cardboard or plastic container with damp sand or sawdust.

DIRECTIONS

Place cookie cutters and sand in front of child.

"What do we usually use these for?"
"What is your favorite shaped cookie?"

"Find all the little cookie cutters and put them together in the sand."
"How many are there?"

"Find the small, medium, and large (hearts) and put them inside each other."

Repeat activity using all the shapes.

Remove cookie cutters and place spoons in front of child.

"Now we'll do something different with the wooden spoons."
"Let's see if you can make them stand up in the sand."
"Now make a row of spoons with the biggest one first and the smallest one last."

"How many spoons are there?"

Remove all but one spoon and place strainer in front of child.

"Shovel some sand inside the strainer."
"Let's see what happens when you shake the strainer."

Encourage child to discuss the pattern made by the sand coming out of the strainer.

Remove strainer and hand child the spatula.

"We can use the spatula to draw shapes in the sand."
"Make a long line."
"Make a circle."

Remove spatula and hand child mold(s).

"We usually make a jello mold(s) out of this, but today we can make a sand mold(s)."

Help child press mold into sand and discuss patterns.

OWL asks:
"If you could keep a mountain of sand in your room, what would you do with it?"

VARIATIONS
Trivets provide another way to promote development of eye-hand control, discrimination of size, shape, numerical concepts, and tactile awareness.
To add more academic interest, number cookie cutters (numerical symbols 1 to 10) can be substituted for shape ones.

PICNIC TIME

FOCUS
○ Stimulate eye-hand coordination
△ Reinforce shape discrimination
△ Emphasize color discrimination
☐ Develop memory for color and number

MATERIALS
Colored plastic knives, forks, and spoons, at least 3 sets of different colors

DIRECTIONS

Place all utensils in front of child.

"Where do we usually find these utensils?"

"There are three different kinds of utensils, what are they called?"

"What is a knife used for?"

"What foods do we eat with a fork?"

"What foods do we eat with a spoon?"

"Find all the utensils that are (yellow) and put them in a pile."

Continue with remaining colors.

"Now let's change the game. This time let's put all the knives together."

"Put all the spoons together."

"Now put all the forks together."

"Let's pretend we're setting the table for you and me. Can you make up a setting for each of us? Be sure each setting has only one color."

"I'm going to change the game again. This time I want you to listen carefully and give me what I ask for."

"Hand me one (red) fork and one (yellow) knife."

Increase difficulty of directions according to child's number and memory skills.

"Hand me one (green) knife and two (orange) forks."

OWL asks:
"What's your favorite food to cut with a knife? Eat with a fork? Eat with a spoon?"

VARIATIONS
Visual memory and sequential skills can be added to this activity for variation. The child observes a pattern of utensils designed by the adult. The length of pattern depends on the child's skill. With eyes closed, the child can be asked to name (from left to right) the objects she saw either by *name* or *color* and *name*. To encourage the child to start from the left, the adult can place a finger under the first item to the left in the pattern. Or, while the child's eyes are closed, the adult can remove one or two object(s) from the pattern. The child looks now at the pattern and attempts to identify and replace the missing object(s).

ALL THAT GLITTERS

FOCUS
△ Establish size discrimination
☐ Label objects
☐ Identify body parts
☐ Reinforce concept of pair

MATERIALS
Discarded costume jewelry (include several pairs of earrings)

DIRECTIONS

Place jewelry in front of child.

"We often wear jewelry because it looks pretty, but today we're going to play some games with it."

Point to each piece one at a time.

"Tell me what this is called."
"What part of your body would you wear it on?" (Prompt as necessary.)

Place a pair of earrings in front of child.

"Here is a pair of earrings. How many are in a pair?"
"Why do we need two earrings?"

Place several pairs of earrings mixed together in front of child.

"Sort this pile into pairs."

Place two necklaces of different lengths in front of child.

"Point to the longer necklace."

"Point to the shorter necklace."

OWL asks:
"Pick up the piece of jewelry you like best and tell me what you like best about it."

58

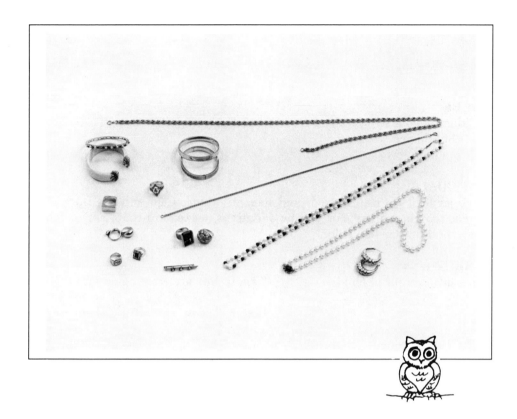

VARIATIONS

The child can also be asked to vary the activity by arranging jewelry in identical patterns to that of the adult. This activity emphasizes sequential visual memory skills. The child observes a short (three to five item) sequence and then closes his eyes. The adult removes one (earring) and asks: "Which piece is missing?" Then hand the item to the child and ask: "Can you put it where it belongs?"

SUGAR AND SPICE

FOCUS
- [ ] Identify colors
- [ ] Label shapes
- [ ] Count objects

MATERIALS

Spice jar lids, assorted in color and size. *Substitute*: Caps and lids from other common kitchen items. For pairing variations, make sure there are matching items, both in size and color.

DIRECTIONS

Place lids in front of child.

"These lids are from spice jars that we use for cooking. Spices make food taste better. Today we will use them to play games."

"Let's see how many colors you can name as I point to each lid."

"Look carefully and tell me if they are all the same shape. What shapes are they?"

"Not all these lids are the same size. First, put all the big lids together and then all the little lids together."

"Now count all the (red) and (yellow) lids for me."
"Please finish this game by counting all the lids."

OWL asks:
"Spices make food taste good. What do you like on your food to make it taste better?"

BELL, BOOK, AND CANDLE

FOCUS
△ Reinforce size discrimination
△ Emphasize directionality
△ Identify colors
□ Count objects
☝ Observe handedness

MATERIALS
Holders, assorted with varying hole sizes
Candles, assortment of various sizes and colors
Book
Bell

DIRECTIONS

Hand the holders one at a time to the child.

"Notice all of these holes that we put candles in. Will your finger fit in there?"
"Count how many holes this one has."
"Now count the holes in each of these holders."

Arrange candle assortment in front of child.

"What color candles do we have here?"
"Are they all the same size?"
"Put all the (green) candles on top of the book."

"Put all the (yellow) candles beside the bell."

Put all candles back together in front of child.

"Are all of the candles the same size?"
"Put the larger candles together in one pile and put all the smaller candles together in another pile."
"Remember how we put puzzles together. Only certain pieces fit in certain holes. This game works the same way. Only certain candles will fit in certain holes."

Place one holder in front of child.
Place another holder in front of child.

"Put the candles that fit properly in this holder."
"Now fill up this holder."

Continue as long as holders and/or interest of child last.

"Let's count how many candles are in each holder."

OWL asks:
"Pick up the bell and ring it once for each candle that will be on your next birthday cake."

HAPPY HOLIDAY GARLANDS

FOCUS
○ Practice eye-hand coordination
△ Reinforce directionality by matching a pattern in a left-to-right sequence
☐ Practice sequential memory
☐ Identify colors
☐ Count objects
☐ Establish concepts of first, next, last

MATERIALS
Two artificial candy garlands, identical
Scissors
Baggies
Cup tree (optional)

PREPARATION
Divide one garland into several lengths of five items each and double knot each end. (Be sure items are in different sequences). Cut remaining part of garland into individual pieces. Put each length and its matching pieces into a baggie. The other garland should be draped on a houseplant or dried arrangement to illustrate its usual function.

DIRECTIONS

Place arrangement with garland in front of child.

"Do you know what garland is?" (A decoration for special occasions.)
"This garland is made of pretend candy. It has Lifesavers and peppermint canes. Wouldn't they be good to eat if they were real?"
"What color are the Lifesavers?"
"What color are the peppermint sticks?"
"What color are the peppermint canes?"

Lay out a length of garland and hand child matching pieces. Be sure child starts sequence from left to right.

"I've cut this garland into little pieces so we can play a game."
"You take these candies and make a line just like mine."

"Now close your eyes and I'll make a new line."

Lay out a new length of garland and hand child matching pieces.

"Look carefully and make the new line the same as mine."

"Now pick up your pieces and hold them in your hand. Look carefully at my line so when I cover it you can remember and make your line just like it."

Cover the line briefly to illustrate and then uncover and let the child look for at least five seconds. Cover again.

"Now let's see if you can remember how to make your line look exactly like mine."

"Count how many pieces are in your line."

Garland length can be reversed to repeat the game.

"Again, hold your pieces in your hand. I will point to the first candy in my line and you put the same candy under mine. Put down your next candy . . . put down your last candy."

°Place cup tree (if available) in front of child. Make loops for the garland lengths with pipe cleaners, string, or the like, and hand to child.

°"Now you can use the garland lengths to decorate your very own tree."

OWL asks:
"If you were a candy cane how would your stripes feel?"

65

KEYS TO THE KINGDOM

FOCUS
○ Practice eye-hand coordination
△ Discriminate sounds
△ Emphasize size discrimination: big, little
□ Establish concepts of more and same
□ Develop memory for numbers
□ Count objects

MATERIALS
Key organizer
Keys, approximately a dozen varying in size and shape
Key rings, several with varying numbers of keys
2 shoelaces (knotted on one end)
Small plastic or metal container
Socks, child's pair

DIRECTIONS

Lay out an assortment of keys in front of child.

"Why do we need keys?"

"We can play some games with these keys."
"Let's make two piles of keys. Put all the big keys in one pile and all the little keys in another pile."

Place container in front of child.

"Pick up two keys. Now pick up two more keys and drop them all in the container."
"Pick up the container and shake it and tell me what you hear."
"Now take the keys out of the container and let's try something else."

Hand the socks to the child.

"Take these socks and drop them in the container."
"What sound do you hear now?"

"Why is it that the keys make a loud sound and the socks don't?"

Begin stringing several keys on one shoelace. (Use no more keys than the child is able to count.) Hand child other shoelace.

"I am going to string some keys on my shoelace. You look at mine so you can put the same number of keys on your shoelace."

Repeat activity. Allow child to study the number of keys on shoelace for at least five seconds and then hide them behind your back.

Place key rings and key organizer in front of child.

Hand rings to child one at a time.

"I want you to remember how many keys are on my shoelace now because I am going to take it away."

"Now string the same number of keys on your shoelace."

"When we have several keys we want to keep together, we put them on a key ring."

"Count how many keys are on this ring and hang them up on the key organizer."

"How many key rings are on the organizer?"

OWL asks:
"What would you do if you had a magic key?"

VARIATIONS

If an assortment of *matching* keys are available, sorting activities, which enhance visual discrimination of size and shape and the concept of a pair, can be incorporated into the directions.

GOODY, GOODY GUMDROPS

FOCUS
△ Match objects in a pattern
☐ Classify objects by size and color
☐ Count objects
☐ Reinforce sequential memory skills

MATERIALS
Jelly beans and gumdrops in varying sizes and colors
Cups or small containers, plastic or paper, in colors that match the candies
Flannel board

DIRECTIONS

Place an assortment of large and small pieces of candy in front of child on a flannel board.

"What do you want to do when you see these candies?"

"Yes, candies are good to eat but we can also play some games with them. After we are finished with the games, you may pick your favorite candies out of the package and eat them."

Place colored containers in front of child.

"Make one pile of large candies and one pile of small candies."

"Now put all the candies in the cups that they match."

"Put all the small (red) candies in the (red) cup and all the large (yellow) candies in the yellow cup."

"Count how many are in each cup."

Make a row of five different colored candies.

"Make a row that looks just like mine."

Remove first row.

"Look carefully at the row you made because I'm going to have you close your eyes and I'll take one away."

"Close your eyes."

Remove one candy and hand to child after he has identified color.

"Now look at the row and tell me what color is missing."
"Put it back where it belongs."

Continue activity, varying the colors.
The child may like to assume the adult role and continue activity.

OWL asks:
(Offer child candies that have not been used in activity.) "What two colors of candy would you like to eat?"
"What do those colors taste like?"

VARIATIONS
To increase the level of difficulty, in place of direction to tell "what color is missing," *substitute* "Can you tell me which (one to three) candies are missing and put them all back where they belong?" Adult can remove an entire row of candy and ask the child to duplicate it from memory according to skill level.

COASTER COUNTERS

FOCUS
○ Practice eye-hand coordination
△ Discriminate color and shape
☐ Identify color and shape
☐ Count objects
☐ Establish concepts of first, second, third, and last

MATERIALS
Potholders, assorted, with loop on one corner
Coasters, round and square, in assorted colors with several color-matched pairs
Shoestring with large knot at one end

PREPARATION
Make sure there are openings in some of the coasters so the child can thread them on the shoestring. You can make holes in paper ones if necessary.

DIRECTIONS

Hand child two potholders.	"Why do we need these close by the stove?"
Hand child two more potholders.	"How many potholders do you have now?"
	"Pick up the (brown) potholder." "Now pick up the (yellow) potholder." "Hand me the (orange) potholder." "Put the (green) potholder on top of the (brown) one."
Hand child a knotted shoestring.	"Let's string these potholders." "Put the (green) one first." "Make the second one (yellow)." "Make the third one (orange)." "What color is the last one?"
Remove potholders and place coasters in front of child.	"Why do we need coasters?"
	"I'm going to put a round coaster here and a square coaster here. You put all the coasters that are the same shape together."
	"How many round coasters are there?" "How many square coasters are there?"

Hand child the shoelace.

"Hand me a pair of (round) (blue) coasters."

"Hand me a pair of (round) (pink) coasters."

"Now find all of the (blue) coasters and make a pile."

"Find all of the (pink) coasters."

"Let's string these coasters using first a (round shape) and then a (square). See what pretty patterns you can make."

OWL asks:
"What's your favorite drink that you would set on this coaster?"

WIND, WAVES, AND WATER

FOCUS
○ Tactile awareness
△ Discriminate top and bottom
☐ Name objects
☐ Identify colors
☐ Identify numbers
  Understand the relationship between water and motion, air currents and motion
  Observe that heavy objects sink and light objects float
  Investigate the physical properties of light and heavy objects

MATERIALS
Large water container (sink, tub, wading pool, etc.)
Foam or plastic coasters, assorted
Sponge objects, assorted
Water toys, assorted (include set of boats)
Plastic containers, small
Rocks, shells, small
Balls, one that floats and one that sinks
Stickers

PREPARATION
Write numbers 1, 2, 3, 4, 5 on stickers and attach to boats and other objects.
Fill tub with lukewarm water.

DIRECTIONS

"Let's swish our hands around in the water. Tell me how that feels."

Place some floating objects other than the boats in tub.

"Let's name all the things that are floating on top of the water."
"What colors are they?"
"What things have gone to the bottom of the tub?"
"What happens to the sponge when you splash the water?"

Hand the child a rock.

"Put the rock in the tub and let's see what happens."

Remove the rock and hand the child a shell.

"Now, let's see what happens when you put the shell in there."

Remove objects and add boats.

"Let's be the wind and blow on the boats."

"Let's blow on boat number 1 (number 2, etc.)."

"Now you blow on the boat that shows your age."

"The waves make things move. Our breath, like the wind, makes thing move. How else can we make things move?"

Hand the child a coaster that will float.

"Take your hand and push the (lily) down to the bottom of the tub."

Hand the child a rock.

"Put this rock in the tub and let's see what happens."

OWL asks:
"If you lived in the water instead of on the land, what would you like to be?"

VARIATIONS

The variation with this activity is accomplished by calling the child's attention to the boats and other objects which display numbers. The child is asked to: "Find two (boats) with the same number; the (boat) with a number that comes after number 4; that comes before number 3." "Put all the (boats) in order, starting with number 1."

PUFF, THE MAGIC DRAGON

FOCUS
- ○ Tactile awareness
- △ Practice directionality: left, right
- △ Emphasize size and color discrimination
- □ Count objects
- □ Establish concepts of small, medium, large, and more
- □ Develop sequential memory

MATERIALS
Powder puffs, assorted, varying in color, design, and size

DIRECTIONS

Hand child the softest powder puff.

"What is this called?" (Prompt, if necessary.)
"What does it feel like?"

Indicate left and right if child is unsure.

"Put all the (pink) powder puffs on your left."
"Put all the (white) powder puffs on your right."
"Count the (pink) ones."
"How many (white) ones are on your right?"
"Are there more (pink) or more (white) powder puffs?"

Depending on age, child may need directions.

"How may more?"
"Now put all the big powder puffs in front of you."
"Give me two of the smallest (pink) powder puffs."

Place a small, medium, and large powder puff in random order in front of child.

"Put these in order with the smallest one first."

Reassemble all the powder puffs together.

"Hand me all the powder puffs that (have patterns)."

Lay out four different puffs in a line.

"Look at this line closely and try to remember what is here. I am going to have you close your eyes and I will take one of the powder puffs away. Then you tell me about the one that is missing."

"Close your eyes."

Remove one powder puff.

Have child replace the missing puff. Repeat as long as interest is maintained.

"Now look and tell me about the one that is missing." (white, big)

OWL asks:
"When you rub this very soft powder puff over your face what does it make you think of?"

HIDDEN TREASURES

FOCUS
○ Practice eye-hand coordination
△ Develop directionality: left, right
△ Reinforce auditory discrimination
□ Practice sequential memory
□ Establish concepts of empty and full

MATERIALS
2 large containers
6 matchboxes, empty
6 film canisters, empty
Assortment of small items such as beads, coins, buttons, candies, etc., that will fit into the matchboxes and canisters
Large piece of paper or material

PREPARATION
Fill three matchboxes and three canisters with small items. Place only like items, e.g., all pennies, all small buttons, all beads, etc., in each canister and box.

DIRECTIONS

Place all canisters and matchboxes in front of child.

"What is usually inside these boxes and these cans?" (Prompt, if necessary.)

"Some of these are empty and some are full. You can find out by shaking them. Don't open them now—we will open them later."

Place one large container to the left of the child and one to the right.

"Put all the empty ones in the bucket on your left side and all the full ones on your right side."

Hand child full canisters and matchboxes, one at a time.

"Shake this close to your ear. What do you hear? What do you think is inside?"

Help child remove lid if necessary and empty contents.

"Let's check and see what's inside. How many (pennies) were there?"

Repeat as long as materials and interest last.

Use two matchboxes and two canisters to make a pattern. Child also has two matchboxes and two canisters. Use a piece of paper to cover up pattern. Repeat, changing order of objects.

"I'm going to use these to make a pattern. I want you to look closely because I'm going to cover it up and have you make one just like it."

Make a row of five objects. Remove one object (or two depending on child's skill level). When child correctly identifies missing object(s), hand to him to replace.

Repeat, changing sequence.

"Now we're going to change the game."
"Look at the row I make very closely. I will cover it up and take something away. You have to tell me what's missing and put it back where it belongs."

OWL asks:
"What are your favorite tiny things that we could put in the matchboxes next time?"

VARIATIONS
Additional ideas to vary this activity include: (1) vary matchbox sizes to develop concept of size discrimination (big, little); (2) change contents in canisters and matchboxes so that one box has only *small* buttons; one canister only *large* buttons; one box has *small, medium, large* coins, beads, etc. Encourage child to label sizes, color, shape of objects used, for example, a small round bead, a brown penny.

HAPPY HOOKING

FOCUS
○ Practice eye-hand coordination
△ Reinforce color discrimination
□ Stimulate spatial awareness: middle, end
□ Count objects

MATERIALS
Length of chain, approximately 1½ ft.
Tacks
Holiday decorations, unbreakable
Infant toys
Hooks, sturdy wire
Pipe cleaner

PREPARATION
Attach hooks and looped pipe cleaners to objects as appropriate.
Tack chain securely to wall in child's room low enough so child can reach.

DIRECTIONS

Place objects in front of child.

"Let's see what things you can hang on this chain to make a pretty decoration."

"When I point to something, you tell me what it is."

"Pick three things that you would like to put on the chain and hand them to me."

Give child one object at a time and point to location.

"Hang the (horse) at this end of the chain."
"Hang the (mouse) at the other end of the chain."
"Hang the (rattle) in the middle."

"Now you pick two more things and hang them wherever you want."

"Count how many things are on the chain."

"Point to the things that have (red) on them."

"Now point to the things that have (white) on them."

Continue with various colors.

OWL asks:
"What other things can you think of that we could hang up here to make a pretty decoration?"

RIBBONS AND BOWS

FOCUS
△ Reinforce color and size discriminations
△ Emphasize spatial awareness: inside, on top of
☐ Identify colors
☐ Count objects
☐ Develop memory skills

MATERIALS
Bows, assorted colors and sizes
Ribbon lengths, one short and one long
Box, with lid

DIRECTIONS

Place bows and empty box in front of child. Allow child to identify color of bow and drop into box.

"What color bow am I putting in this box?"
"You find all the other (red) bows and put them inside of the box."

Repeat until all bows have been put in box.

"Now look in the box and take out all the (blue) bows."
"How many (blue) bows do you have?"

Repeat with other colors as long as interest lasts.

Place box with lid on in front of child

"Put all the little (white) bows on top of the box."

"Put all the big (orange) bows on top of the box."

"How many bows are there altogether?"

Remove box and bows, keep lid.

Place ribbons in front of child.

"Point to the long ribbon."
"Point to the short ribbon."

Cover ribbons with lid and remove one.

"Which ribbon is left?"

OWL asks:
"If you wrapped a package as big as your bed, how many bows would you use?"

VARIATIONS

Two visual memory skill activities are emphasized by the following directions: "Look carefully at the pile of bows I will put in front of you. Close your eyes and I'll take one away. Which color bow is missing?" "Look closely again at the ribbons I have placed in a line. I'm going to cover them up (sheet of paper) and I want you to make a ribbon line that looks just the same as mine."

PLAYFUL POUCH

FOCUS
○ Eye-hand coordination
△ Reinforce auditory discrimination
□ Label objects
□ Count objects

MATERIALS
Drawstring pouch, small, such as used for bubble gum bits or jacks
Assortment of small objects to fit into pouch (e.g., bottle caps, coins, macaroni, buttons, jacks, etc.)
Flannel board (optional)

DIRECTIONS

Lay out groups of items on flannel board or other flat surface.

"Look at these things I have put on (the flannel board). Can you tell me what is in each group?"
"I want you to close your eyes and I will put something in the pouch."

Give closed pouch you have filled to child and encourage her to shake it.

"Can you guess what's in the pouch by shaking it?"
"Let's open it and see if you guessed right."
"How many (pennies) were in there?"

Continue with new objects as long as interest lasts.

Game can be reversed so that child fills pouch and adult guesses.

"Now it's your turn to fill the pouch and I will close my eyes."

OWL asks:
"If we used your pillowcase for a pouch,
what could you put in it?"

UP, UP, AND AWAY

FOCUS
△ Match objects in a pattern
△ Reinforce color discrimination
△ Emphasize size discrimination
☐ Count objects
☐ Identify color
☐ Practice memory skills

MATERIALS
Balloons, varying in size and color. Make sure there are at least five matching pairs. (Don't blow up the balloons until the end of the activity.)

DIRECTIONS

Place balloons in front of child.	"We usually have balloons for special occasions. Can you remember where you've seen them?" (Prompt, if necessary.)
	"Hand me all the (orange) balloons." "How many big (orange) balloons are there?" "How many small (orange) balloons are there?" "How many (orange) balloons are there altogether?"
Repeat with other colors.	
Make pattern with four balloons and give child matching set.	"I will make a pattern with my balloons. Tell me what color I am putting down. You take these and make one just like mine."
Repeat as long as interest lasts.	
Make pattern and hand child set of balloons.	"Now we're going to change the game. I'm going to make another pattern. You look at it very closely because I will take one balloon away later when you close your eyes. Look closely."
Remove one balloon.	"Now close your eyes." "Open your eyes. Use one of your balloons to make the pattern the way it was."

Repeat as long as interest lasts.

"Pick your three favorite colors and we'll blow them up."

OWL asks:

"What special times do balloons make you think of?"

RED HEARTS

FOCUS
○ Practice eye-hand coordination
△ Develop color discrimination
△ Match objects in a pattern
□ Count objects

MATERIALS
Playing cards, discarded deck
Shoestring, knotted at one end
Paper punch
Red Hots

PREPARATION
Use the 2 through 10 of hearts and clubs. Cut cards so that only the number, not the symbol at upper left-hand corner shows. Cut strip from right-hand side to remove symbol and number. Punch a hole at the top of each card.

DIRECTIONS

	"Adults play lots of games with cards. I've made up some special cards for us so we can play some special games."
Place 2, 3, 4, and 5 of clubs in front of child and point to clubs.	"These little black things are called clubs."
Point to number.	"Look at this number and tell me how many clubs are on this card."
	"This number always tells how many clubs are on the card."
Put Red Hots in front of child.	"We're going to play a game where we match a Red Hot to each club. Put one Red Hot in the middle of each club. How many will you need for this card?"
Continue with remaining cards. (With older child add more cards to sequence.)	
Remove Red Hots.	
String 2 of clubs on shoelace and hand to child.	"If we string these cards in order, which one comes next?" "Tell me the number as you string it."
Continue with remaining cards. (With older child add more cards to sequence.) Remove cards from string.	

Place sequence of hearts in front of child.

"Those cards were black and called clubs, these cards are red."

Point to heart.

"Can you tell me what this is?"
"Yes, these cards are called hearts."

Hand clubs to child.

"Find the black two and put it under the red two."

"How many hearts are there?
"How many clubs are there?"
"How many hearts and clubs are there altogether?"
"That's right, two and two are four."

Continue through sequence as ability level of child allows. Younger child will only be able to match.

OWL asks:
"What game of cards do you like to play best?"

THE PARTY'S OVER

FOCUS
△ Match by color
△ Match a pattern in a left-to-right sequence
△ Emphasize directionality
△ Match a pattern both left-to-right and up and down
☐ Reinforce concept of same
☐ Count objects

MATERIALS
Paper tablecloth for child's party
Matching napkins
Scissors
Cardboard sections
Scotch tape

PREPARATION
From tablecloth: Cut out sequences of items that vary in number from two to six. Tape to cardboard. Make three individual cards identical to each item used in the sequence cards. Separate into three sets.
From napkins: Cut out as many different sequences as possible and attach to cardboard. Use both vertical and horizontal sequences.

DIRECTIONS

"Do you remember the tablecloth we used at your party? Do you remember what pictures were on it?"

"I have made a game for you out of the leftover cloth and napkins."

Using large items from table-cloth, lay out one set of cards with individual items in front of child. Hand child the other two sets of individual items.

"Let's match up our cards. Put the cards that are the same as mine on top."

"Count how many piles we have."

Place larger card with se-quenced items in front of child.

"Here is a card with (two) items on it. Look at the card and find two items from your piles that are the same color. Make your picture below mine."

When child has finished, return individual items to piles.

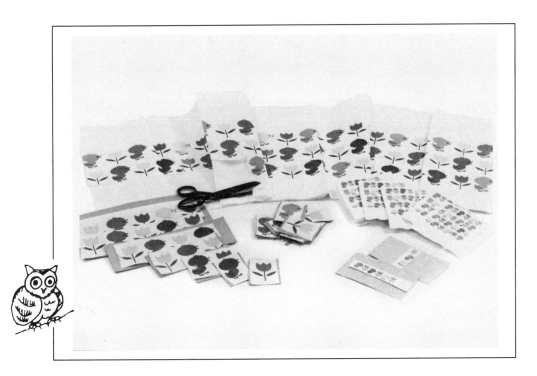

Continue activity using longer sequences. For older children several cards can be used together to lengthen the sequence.

Using smaller patterns from napkins, lay out one vertical sequence and one horizontal sequence.

Repeat as above.

"Now the game is harder. You need to match my picture going across and also going down."

OWL asks:
"Who are you going to invite to your next party?"

PAINT THE TOWN

FOCUS
○ Practice eye-hand coordination
△ Emphasize visual discrimination of light and dark
△ Stimulate color discrimination
□ Develop concept of pair
□ Count objects

MATERIALS
Paint and vinyl samples (get at least 2 of each color paint sample), with holes punched at the top. *Substitute:* Fabric scraps and wallpaper samples
3 shoelaces
Electric outlet insulators

DIRECTIONS

Place paint samples in front of child.

"These paint samples came from the store. Usually we use them to show us what colors we could paint our house. Today we will play some games with them."

"I want you to make pairs of each color and put them together."

Hand child a shoelace knotted at one end.

"Now you string these to make a pretty pattern using one of each color."

Copy child's pattern.

"I will use the other part of the pair and make a pattern just like yours."

Remove paint samples and place vinyl samples in front of child.

"This time make one pile of (light) colors and one pile of (dark) colors."

Hand child a shoelace knotted at one end.

"Take this shoelace and string one (light) and one (dark)."
"Now string two (light) and two (dark)."

Increase difficulty of directions according to child's memory and number skills ability.

Remove vinyl samples and place insulator pieces and shoelace in front of child.

Hand one insulator piece to child.

"This piece has two slits in it. Can you find them?"

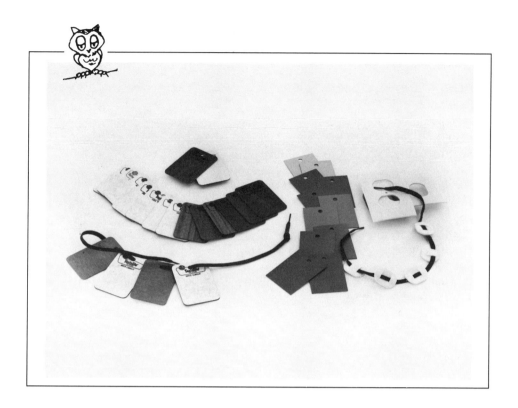

Put one piece on shoelace and hand to child.

"These are going to be harder to string, so I will show you how."

"Count the pieces as you put them on the shoelace."

"Now pull them off the shoelace and count them as you take them off."

OWL asks:

"If it were time to paint your room a new color, which one of these colors would you pick?"

GIFTS THAT KEEP ON GIVING

FOCUS
△ Sort by design
△ Sort by color
☐ Count objects
☐ Sort by category
☐ Label objects
☐ Identify colors
☐ Develop concept of first

MATERIALS
Paper clips, scissors, glue, cardboard
6 paper sacks
Gift wrapping paper, assorted solids and patterns (Try to collect paper with clear and appealing designs)

PREPARATION
Have large assortment of various types of paper cut into pieces the child can easily handle.
Cut out and attach to cardboard a set of items in the same category such as food, toys, people, flowers, etc.

DIRECTIONS

Place assortment of gift wrapping scraps in front of child.

"Why do we call this paper gift wrapping?"
"Do you remember what was in the last package that you unwrapped?"
"Let's make two piles of gift wrapping paper."
"Put all the paper that has just one color in this pile."
"Put all the paper that has a design or picture in this pile."
"What colors are in the first pile?"

Hand child a piece of gift wrapping that depicts an activity. Continue using new pictures as long as interest is sustained.

"Tell me what you think is going on in this picture."

Hand child the set of items that have been attached to cardboard. Have three paper sacks open in front of child. Attach one picture to each sack with a paper clip.
Change pictures to vary activity.

"Let's pretend we are at the (grocery store)."
"Tell me the names of these (fruits)."
"Put all the (lemons) in this sack and all the (strawberries) in the other sack."

Remove items from sacks and return to child.

"Now let's change the game. Put all the (red fruits) in this sack and all the (yellow fruits) in the other sack."

"How many (red fruits) are there?"
"How many (yellow fruits) are there?"

OWL asks:
"If you received a package as big as the refrigerator, what gift would you like to find inside?"

VARIATIONS

Empty seed packets can be substituted as fruit or vegetable pictures and attached to individual lunch sacks for pretend fruit or vegetable bins.

The "crayon" gift paper cards could be placed in "pretend crayon boxes" matching the picture on top of the box (just as the picture cards were attached to sacks). This same procedure can be repeated with each theme from *suitable* gift paper, e.g., toys, people, flowers, a special event, etc.

Another variation of the activity is to place an assortment of gift wrapping paper scraps which vary by colors, designs, and patterns in front of the child. The child can sort the scraps according to directions: "Find all the papers with just one color"; "Find all the papers with stripes"; and so on.

REMEMBRANCE OF THINGS PAST

FOCUS
- □ Develop vocabulary of holiday names
- □ Classify by category
- △ Identify colors
- □ Count objects
- △ Establish size discrimination
- □ Reinforce memory skills

MATERIALS

Holiday cards (Christmas, birthday, Valentine's Day, etc.)—approximately 20. Select assortment of cards that have appealing, clear pictures that contrast sharply with background of the card.

DIRECTIONS

Place several cards that represent a particular holiday in front of child.

"What do these cards make you think of?"
"Which picture do you like best?"
"Tell me what's going on in that picture."

Stand up several cards from different categories.

"I am going to put a card with a (candle) on it here. You find all the other cards with (candles) on them and put them in front of my card."

Continue with new categories as long as interest is sustained.

Have child focus on one category. Verbally describe a picture and have child locate it.

"Find the card that has (red, yellow, and blue bells)."
"Count the (bells)."

Continue using different categories.

Place four of the category piles in front of the child.

"Tell me what we have in these four different piles."

This activity is played like the game of concentration. It may take child several trials to understand the point of the game.

"You hide your eyes and I'm going to turn one of the piles over."
"Can you remember what was in that pile?"

Continue with each category pile.

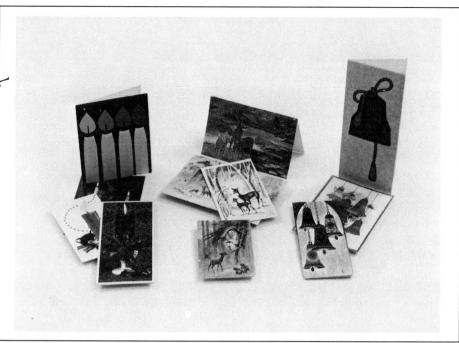

OWL asks:
"What holiday do you like best? Can you tell me why it's your favorite?"

VARIATIONS
Variation of the above activity can be accomplished by including one to three types of holiday cards. The child then sorts the birthday cards from the Christmas cards and the Valentine cards into appropriate piles.

SILLY SEALS

FOCUS
○ Practice eye-hand coordination
△ Establish spatial awareness
□ Label objects
□ Classify by category
□ Count objects

MATERIALS
Holiday and stationery seals. (When necessary, attach seals to cardboard backing)
Envelopes

DIRECTIONS

Place seals in categories in front of child.

"Let's see how many different ways we can play with these seals."

Point to each category.

"Tell me what we call these." (Prompt as necessary.)

Mix two categories together and hand child an envelope.

"Find all the (flowers) and put them in this envelope."

"How many (flowers) do you think are in your envelope?"
"Now take them out of the envelope and count them as you do."

Repeat activity by mixing new categories.

Place large seals in front of child.

"Now I want you to find all of the seals that have (red) on them and put them in the envelope."

Repeat with other colors as long as interest is maintained.

Place a sequence of three seals in front of child. One seal should be in a different position than the other two.

"Which seal is different?"
"Why?"
"Can you make it look the same as the others?"

Repeat activity. Child may enjoy reversing roles with the adult.

OWL asks:
"Look around the room and tell me what else besides the seals would fit into our envelopes."

VARIATIONS

Once the large seals have been used, the outlines can provide an opportunity to reinforce eye-hand coordination by having the child trace the outline with a dark or contrasting felt-tip pen.

Another variation for eye-hand coordination development would be to have the child string the seals that have been attached to cardboard using a shoelace. The only preparation would be using a paper punch for each card.

An additional variation is to remove (three) seals from the seal sheet making certain that (three) seals still remain. Then ask: "How many mice do you see?" "How many are missing?"

If seals have been purchased in boxes, another variation is possible. Place two to four empty boxes in front of the child. The child is required to open boxes carefully and place inside each box the seal that appears on the top of each box. Concepts of "open" and "shut" can be emphasized.

PAPER CHASE

FOCUS
△ Establish directionality: in front of
△ Reinforce size discrimination
☐ Count objects
☐ Identify colors

MATERIALS
Paper products (stationery, note pads, napkins, etc.) depicting a common theme such as ladybugs, owls, frogs, flowers, etc. Images should be bright, clear, and appealing. A collection of cancelled stamps (trimmed from envelopes with 1/4 in. margin) provides a good substitute for or addition to the materials already listed.

DIRECTIONS

Place items in front of child.
Point to (ladybug).

"Do you know what these are called?"
"If they were real, where would you find them?"
"Today we're going to play some games with these (ladybugs)."

"Put the (napkin) with small (ladybugs) in front of you."

"Put the (napkin) with large (ladybugs) in front of me."

"How many large (ladybugs) are there?"
"How many small (ladybugs) are there?"
"How many (ladybugs) are there altogether?"

"Find the biggest (ladybug). What color(s) is it?"
"Count how many (dots) it has."
"What color are they?"

"Find the next biggest (ladybug). Count how many (dots) it has."

Continue as objects allow and interest holds.

OWL asks:
"What is the biggest number you can think of?"

To Our Readers

The authors sincerely request that you share the variations and/or new ideas for activities that evolve as you and your child work together.
Send them to:

        Judith S. McClure
        Box 6084
        Denver, CO 80206

About the Authors

Claudette Stock, M.A., is an author and educator who is trained and experienced in the areas of preschool, learning-disabled, and multi-handicapped children. Her career has encompassed teaching in the Denver public school system; Preschool Instructor at the University of Kansas Medical Center, Children's Rehabilitation Unit; Preschool Education Director at John F. Kennedy Child Development Center, Denver, Colorado; Education Consultant to Psychiatric and Guidance Clinic in Denver; Educational Specialist with public schools, Craig, Colorado, Jefferson County and Montrose, Colorado. Ms. Stock is the author of two books: *The Minimal Brain Dysfunction Child* and *Learning Tasks for the Pre-Academic Child*.

Judith S. McClure, Ph.D., is an educator and educational psychologist. She is currently an Associate Professor of Education at Regis College, Denver, Colorado, where she teaches courses in Adult Life-Cycles, Educational Psychology, Child Development, and Early Childhood Education. She has also taught in public schools and at the University of Colorado Graduate School of Education. In addition, she has established learning centers and consulted in educational evaluation, learning disabilities, and parenting education.

In 1967, the authors established the John F. Kennedy Child Development Center Nursery School at the University of Colorado Medical Center. They have subsequently collaborated on a number of projects, including workshops and classes in parenting.